Savvy

CRAFTY CREATIONS

Knitting Projects You'll Purl Over

by Kelly McClure

Raintree is an imprint of Capstone Global Library Limited, a company incorporated in England and Wales having its registered office at Meridian House, Sandy Lane West, Littlemore, Oxford, OX4 6LB – Registered company number: 6695582

www.raintree.co.uk
myorders@raintree.co.uk

Editorial Credits
Editor: Marissa Bolte
Designer: Juliette Peters
Photo stylist: Sarah Schuette
Scheduler: Marcy Morin
Production specialist: Kathy McColley
Project creators: Kelly McClure and Stephanie Miller

ISBN 978 1 4747 4557 4
22 21 20 19 18
10 9 8 7 6 5 4 3 2 1

British Library Cataloguing in Publication Data
A full catalogue record for this book is available from the British Library.

Acknowledgements
All images by Capstone Studio/Karon Dubke except Shutterstock: littleny, cover (bottom), steveball, cover (top)

Printed and bound in India.

Contents

Let's knit!

Knitting is a magical method that uses string and needles to create loops. These loops interlock to create fabric. This very portable hobby has infinite possibilities.

Although evidence is scarce, we know that knitting has been around for at least 10,000 years. Early humans used to spin yarn using stones as weights. The first known knitted socks were made in Egypt. Later in history, knitting became a pastime for shepherds. They learned to knit on stilts so that they could keep an eye on their flocks of sheep.

These days, knitting is becoming more popular. It is a great way to create something that is original and personal to you. Knitted items make impressive gifts for friends and family. It does take some practice, but once you get going you will find that it's hard to put your needles down!

Yarn

Yarn can be made from all kinds of fibre. Some yarn comes from animals, some from plants and some are synthetic.

The most popular fibre for knitting is wool that comes from sheep, but there is also wool that comes from alpaca, llama, musk ox, rabbit (angora), goat (cashmere), camel, possum and silkworm (silk). Some people even spin wool from their dog's fur! Plant-based yarns include cotton, linen (from flax), hemp, soy and bamboo.

Acrylic (synthetic) yarns are affordable and available in many different colours and textures. These won't be as warm as wool fibre, but they are a great choice for beginners. You will want to choose yarns that are smooth and simple when you are starting out. Try to avoid anything that is too fuzzy or frilly until you have practised a bit.

A US organization called the *Craft Yarn Council* created a standard system to organize yarns by weight and thickness. This is called the Yarn Standard Weight System.

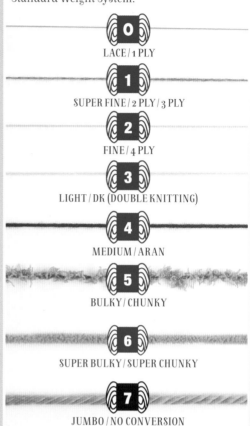

0 — LACE / 1 PLY

1 — SUPER FINE / 2 PLY / 3 PLY

2 — FINE / 4 PLY

3 — LIGHT / DK (DOUBLE KNITTING)

4 — MEDIUM / ARAN

5 — BULKY / CHUNKY

6 — SUPER BULKY / SUPER CHUNKY

7 — JUMBO / NO CONVERSION

ball of sheep yarn

ball of goat yarn

hank of llama yarn

6

bullet skein

umbrella swift

Yarn comes in many forms: balls, skeins or cakes. Often, your yarn comes ready to use. Most yarn comes in a "bullet skein" or ball – which, surprisingly, don't really look like balls at all!

It's a good idea to fish around through the hole in your ball to find the end of the yarn, known as the "tail". Pull this out and let the ball unravel as you knit. If your yarn is wound into a cake, you should also pull it from the centre.

If your yarn comes in a skein (also called a "hank"), ask the shop where you bought it if they can wind it into a cake for you using a swift. If not, find a partner who can hold the big loop of yarn on his or her hands while you wind it into a ball. You can also use the back of a chair, or your knees.

7

Tools

The first knitting needles were probably made from sharpened sticks. Today you can buy needles made of plastic, metal, bamboo or wood, to name a few materials. There are also many different styles of needles:

1 **Straight needles** have points on one end and stoppers on the other so your stitches don't slide off. They come in different lengths and are good for knitting flat items, like scarves.

2 **Circular needles** are joined with a flexible cord and are perfect for knitting either round items like a hat, or flat items, like a shawl. They are also ideal for wide items, like blankets, since you can buy them in many different lengths.

Knitting needle conversion chart

METRIC	US
2 mm	0
2.25 mm	1
2.5 mm	-
2.75 mm	2
3 mm	-
3.25 mm	3
3.5 mm	4
3.75 mm	5
4 mm	6
4.5 mm	7
5 mm	8
5.5 mm	9
6 mm	10
6.5 mm	10 1/2
7 mm	-
7.5 mm	-
8 mm	11
9 mm	13
10 mm	15

Needles come in sizes ranging from very skinny to very thick. Each country has its own classification system. You will see metric, European and US sizes and numbers, so make sure you are selecting the correct set!

3 Double-pointed needles have points at both ends and are usually used to knit small items in the round, like socks or mittens.

Other tools used for knitting include scissors, a tape measure and stitch markers.

4 Stitch markers are used to show where the beginning of your round is. They can also mark between sections, or just mark one side of your fabric. They come in lots of different styles. If you aren't sure what to choose, you can just use a safety pin (or tie on a loop of scrap yarn) to start.

5 Sometimes a crochet hook can come in handy, especially for fixing mistakes and weaving in ends (tails).

6 Another useful tool is a large sewing needle, sometimes called a tapestry needle. This can be used to sew pieces together or to weave in tails when you are finished with your project.

How to read a pattern

Knitters use code to simplify a pattern. It works the same way as any other code: you are given a symbol or abbreviation and a chart or "key" is provided to explain the meaning of the symbols. For example, if your pattern says "st", it really means "stitch". Your pattern should always give you all the information you need to complete the project.

It's a good idea to try and read a pattern all the way through before you begin, even if most of it doesn't make sense straight away. Like most crafts, just take it one step at a time. Before you know it, you will be able to read a knitting pattern like it's a secret code!

Abbreviations

approx = approximately

beg = beginning

BO = bind/cast off

CO = cast on

dpns = double-pointed needles

K = knit

K2tog = knit two stitches together

m = marker

P = purl

PM = place marker

rep = repeat

rem = remain(ing)

rev St st - reverse stocking stitch

rnd(s) = round(s)

RS = right side

st(s) = stitch(es)

St st = stocking stitch

WS = wrong side

YO = yarn over

How to read a yarn label

Your yarn label will give you a great deal of information. Some of it might look hard to understand at first. But this info can be important to help you choose the correct yarn for your pattern.

1. BRAND: Yarn always has a company name and a yarn name. For example, the company name is Red Heart and the yarn name is Super Saver.

2. THICKNESS: It is really important to use the same yarn thickness as the pattern. If it's too thick or thin, your project will turn out too big or too small. In order to help with this, yarn is categorized by thickness: Lace, Sock (also called fingering), DK (double knitting), Worsted, Aran, Chunky and Super Chunky. Sometimes, your yarn will have a number that corresponds to the weight category from 0 (Lace/1 ply) to 6 (Super Bulky/Chunky). See the chart on page 6.

3. NEEDLES: Another thing to consider is the size of the needles you are using. If you don't use the correct needle size, your project might be too big or too small.

4. TENSION Your yarn label will suggest what size needles to use to get an average "tightness" or "tension". Usually there is a little chart on your yarn label explaining how many stitches you should get with a specific size needle. This is just an average, but it is a good indication of how many stitches you should get when using that recommended yarn and needle size.

5. FIBRE: Your label will tell you exactly what kind of fibre makes up your yarn. Sometimes it's a few different kinds of fibres mixed together! Your label should also include washing instructions for that fibre. Hand knit items should always be washed by hand, not put in the washing machine.

6. WEIGHT: Your label will also tell you how much your yarn weighs. Often, yarn is sold in 50 grams (1.75 ounces) or 100 grams (3.5 ounces). The 100-gram size will allow you to make most small accessories like hats or gloves.

7. LENGTH: The label will also tell you how many metres are in your ball. Keep in mind that different types of fibres weigh different amounts. 100 metres of sheep's wool, which is light and fluffy, will weigh less than 100 metres of silk, which is often dense and heavy.

8. COLOUR: Your label will also tell you the colour. This might be a name or a number. There will also be a Lot Number, and a Dye Number. If you are using more than one ball of the same colour, you will want to have the same Lot and Dye Numbers for all the balls so that the colour matches exactly. Buying all the yarn you need for a project at the same time will ensure consistency.

How to knit

Knitting is usually done in three parts. First, you cast stitches onto your needles. Then you knit your fabric. Finally, you bind off your stitches. If you didn't bind off your stitches, your loops would unravel.

Don't forget: the first row of any pattern is always the hardest. Once you have a few rows completed, it will get much easier.

How to make a slip knot

The slip knot is the first thing you do before you start any project. Most patterns don't even include this in the instructions because it is assumed that you already know this.

1. To make a slip knot to fit the needle, shape the yarn like a pretzel.

2. Slip the needle into the pretzel and pull down on both ends of the yarn to tighten the knot.

Cast on

Start with a slip knot. Leave a tail of about 20 cm and just let it dangle while you knit. Place this slip knot on one of your needles and pull it tight, but not too tight. You should be able to slide it easily up and down the needle.

Now, hold the needle in your left hand like you would hold a bike handle. Using your right hand, twist your live yarn (not the tail) to make a loop and place this loop on the needle next to the slip knot. Pull the yarn gently so the stitch is cuddled right up next to the slip knot (but not too tight!). Now, you have two stitches on your needle.

Continue making loops with your right hand and placing them on the needle next to the other stitches until you have the correct number.

Now you are ready to knit!

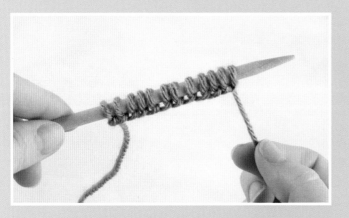

Knit stitch

There are really only two kinds of stitches: knits and purls. Now, we will cover the knit stitch.

Tip:

To hold the yarn, twist it around the little finger on your right hand. Have the strand run under your ring and middle finger, and then over your index finger. This will give your yarn a bit of tension as you knit and will help keep your stitches even. It may feel awkward at first, but keep practising! Soon, you will be able to just flick your index finger in order to wrap the yarn around the needle.

To begin, you might find it easier to just hold the yarn between your thumb and index finger.

To start the knit stitch, you should have the live yarn (the strand that comes from the ball) in the back. The right needle should be in front of the live yarn.

To work the knit stitch, you will insert your right needle into the next stitch on your left needle from front to back and left to right. Make sure you are inserting the right needle into the front leg of the stitch (as it comes over the needle towards you) and not the back leg. Inserting it into the back of the stitch will cause it to twist.

While your right needle is still in the stitch, wrap your live yarn around the right needle anti-clockwise: towards you and between the needles. You should have wrapped the yarn right around the right needle.

"Hook" the wrapped yarn with the right needle and pull it through the stitch. Push the stitch off the left needle and let it drop. You should now have a stitch on your right needle and you are ready to work the next stitch.

Purl stitch

Purls are actually the reverse side of a knit stitch. If you look at the backside of a knit stitch, it will look like a purl stitch. Purls look like little bumps, while knit stitches have a smoother look.

To start the purl stitch, you should have your live yarn in the front. The right needle should be behind the live yarn.

To work the purl stitch, you will insert your right needle into the next stitch on your left needle from right to left. Make sure you are inserting the right needle into the front leg of the stitch (as it comes over the needle towards you) and not the back leg. Inserting it into the back of the stitch will cause it to twist.

While your right needle is still in the stitch, wrap your live yarn around the right needle anti-clockwise: towards you and between the needles. You should have wrapped the yarn right around the right needle.

"Hook" the wrapped yarn with the right needle and pull it through the stitch. Push the stitch off the left needle and let it drop. You should now have a stitch on your right needle and you are ready to work the next stitch.

Increase

There are many ways to increase the number of stitches that you have. Here, we will cover two easy methods. In the Rainbow Blanket pattern, you will also learn a third method called a Yarn Over.

 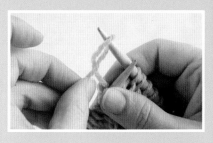

1 When you come to the point in your fabric where you have to make your increase, simply use the live strand to cast on an extra loop (just like you did for the cast on).

Twist the live yarn into a loop and place it on the right needle, pulling it snug. You now have an extra stitch on the right needle.

2 When you come to the point in your fabric where you have to make your increase, use your right needle to pick up an extra stitch from the row below. If you pull your needles apart slightly, you will see a horizontal strand running between the right and left needle. Insert your right needle under this strand from front to back. Wrap your yarn and knit the stitch as you usually would. You now have an extra stitch on the right needle.

Decrease

There are also many ways to decrease, but here we will only cover the most common one.

Knit two together (K2tog)

Insert your right needle into the second stitch on the left needle (skipping one stitch) as you would to knit it (from left to right and front to back in the front leg of the stitch).

Next, insert your needle into the first stitch on the left needle in the same way.

Wrap your yarn around the right needle as you would to knit.

Pull the strand through both stitches and let them drop off the left needle. You should now have one stitch on the right needle.

Tip:

This is exactly the same way you would make a knit stitch, but you are doing it with two stitches instead of one.

Tension

An important part of knitting is called "tension". What this refers to is the tightness of your stitches. If your stitches are too loose, your fabric will be floppy and thin. If your stitches are too tight, your fabric will be stiff and thick. Sometimes you want a little bit of "drape" or floppiness – usually for a scarf or a sweater. You also sometimes might want to have a stiff fabric, for things like mittens or a hat.

Another thing to think about when it comes to tension is your pattern specifications. If you are making a hat and your stitches are too loose, the hat might turn out to be too big. If your stitches are too tight, the hat will be too small.

If you are worried that your tension might not match what your yarn label or pattern tells you, you can knit up a little swatch to get an idea of how close you are. Some knitters know they knit a bit tightly, so they will choose a slightly larger needle than what is recommended. Some knitters knit a bit loosely, so they would choose a smaller needle to make sure their project ends up being the correct size.

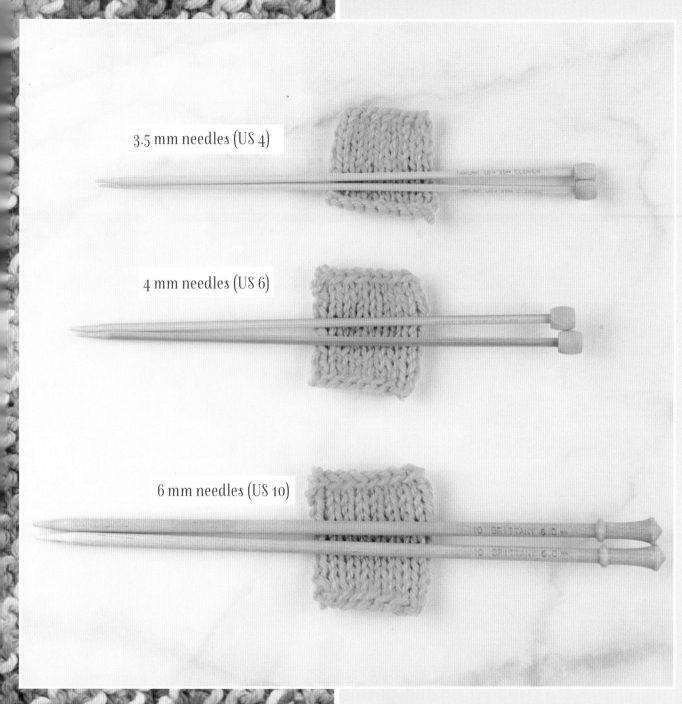

3.5 mm needles (US 4)

4 mm needles (US 6)

6 mm needles (US 10)

A good rule of thumb is to make sure that your needles are sliding easily through the stitches. If they are too tight, it might feel hard to move your stitches along the needle. If they are too loose, your needle will fall out. Try to relax your hands and practise, practise, practise! It takes time to develop a "good" tension so that your stitches are even.

Bind/cast off

Binding off is simply a way to finish off your fabric so your stitches don't unravel. If you are knitting a piece of flat fabric, this step is essential. If you are making a hat in the round that gradually gets smaller at the top, you will not need to bind off. Binding off is also called "casting off".

1. Knit two stitches.

2. Insert your left needle into the first stitch that you knit (on the right needle) from left to right in the front leg of the loop.

3. Pull it up and over the next stitch on the right needle and let it drop off the needle. You will now have one stitch on the right needle.

4. Knit one stitch.

5. Repeat steps 2-4 until you have one stitch left. Cut your yarn and pull the tail right through the last loop. Pull it tight.

Weaving in ends

When you are finished with your project, you will have at least two tails hanging from the fabric. Some knitters choose to tie a knot onto the fabric and then weave in the tails, but this is not necessary (unless your yarn is really slippery).

With the wrong side of the fabric facing out use either a crochet hook or a sewing needle to "weave" the tail into the fabric on the wrong side, climbing along the backs of the stitches. If done correctly, you won't even see this tail on the right side of the fabric.

The best way to lock this tail into place so that it doesn't come undone is to go first in one direction and then turn and come back in the other. Tug on your fabric a bit so that your woven tail sits comfortably. If you pull the tail too tight, it will make the fabric pucker. Snip your tail, leaving a tiny bit of length so it doesn't come loose.

What to do when you make a mistake

Everyone makes mistakes – even experienced knitters! – so don't feel upset when it happens to you. Making mistakes is the best way to learn and is part of the process. There are a few ways to fix mistakes, but it's up to you how far you want to go to fix them. Sometimes a little mistake can add some charm to your project. There are tips throughout the book to help you if you need a quick fix.

Garter stitch cowl

This bulky cowl is a good way to practise your knit stitch. When you knit every row in a flat project, it is called "garter stitch". If you aren't ready to change colours yet, you can definitely make it all in one colour and it will still look fabulous!

Materials

less than 260 m / 250 g of a chunky yarn in three colours

10 mm straight or circular needles

large sewing needle

Skills

cast on, knit stitch, bind off, sewing ends together (optional)

Work back and forth (flat).

1 Cast on 15 stitches.

2 Knit 30 rows (knitting every stitch and then turning the fabric at the end of every row). You should see 15 bumpy ridges.

3 Cut the first colour, leaving a 25.5-cm tail. You can weave it in later. If you are making the cowl in one colour, you can just keep knitting!

4 Begin the next row with a new colour, leaving a 25.5-cm tail when you start knitting. Knit 30 rows.

5 Continue knitting 30 rows of each colour until you have made two "squares" of each (six total). Your cowl should measure approximately 1.3m.

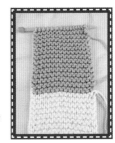

6 Bind off all of your stitches loosely. Cut yarn, leaving a 76-cm tail.

7 Sew the two ends together, making sure it isn't twisted. You can also leave the ends un-sewn and wear it as a scarf!

8 Weave in all tails on the "wrong side".

Tip:

The leftover yarn is used to make the Garter Stitch Headband on the next spread.

Garter stitch headband

This simple headband will be perfect to pair with your Garter Stitch Cowl! It is knit with slightly smaller needles, but is still very stretchy.

Materials

28 m / 25 g of a chunky yarn in three colours

8 mm straight or circular needles

large sewing needle

Skills

cast on, knit stitch, bind off, sewing ends together

Tip:
You should place a stitch marker or safety pin on the "right side" of the fabric as you did with the cowl.

Work back and forth (flat).

1 Cast on 8 stitches.

2 Knit 20 rows (knitting every stitch and then turning the fabric at the end of every row). You should see 10 bumpy ridges.

3 Cut the first colour, leaving a 25.5-cm tail. You can weave it in later.

4 Begin knitting with the next colour, leaving a 25.5-cm tail when you start knitting. Knit 20 rows.

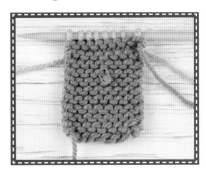

5 Cut the second colour, leaving a 25.5-cm tail. Knit 20 rows with the third colour.

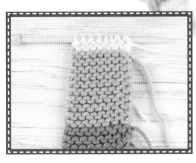

Your headband should measure approximately 45 to 50 cm.

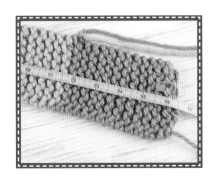

6 Bind off all of your stitches loosely. Cut yarn leaving a 38-cm tail.

7 Sew the two ends together, making sure the headband isn't twisted. Weave in all tails on the "wrong side".

25

I-cord necklaces and bracelets

These delicate accessories are fun to make and fun to wear. They are made with double pointed needles but are worked back and forth with a special technique that is very easy!

Materials

less than 100 m / 25 g of a DK-weight yarn in three colours

Two sets of 3 1/2 mm double-pointed needles

large sewing needle

Skills

cast on, knit stitch, bind off, sewing ends together

1 Cast on 4 stitches.

2 Knit 4 stitches.

3 Do not turn your needle so that the wrong side faces you. The right side should still face you. Slide your stitches to the other end of the needle. This is now your left needle. Your live strand should be on the left side.

4 Pull the live strand tightly around the back and knit 4 stitches again.

Repeat steps 3-4.

5 You will see after a few rows that you are making a skinny "rope" (also called an i-cord). Bracelets should be 15 to 16.5 cm long. For necklaces, you'll need three lengths – 45, 55 and 60 cm. When your cord is to your desired length, bind off all 4 stitches.

6 Sew the ends of the i-cord together and pull the tails through the middle of the i-cord and trim.

Slouchy hat

For this pattern, we will start to use more abbreviations. You can look them up on page 10. This easy-to-make hat comes in two sizes, so pick the one that fits you (or your friend!) the best.

Materials

143.5 m / 100 g of an aran-weight yarn

6 mm 40.5-cm circular needles

stitch marker

large sewing needle

Skills

cast on, knit stitch, bind off, sewing ends together

Work in the rnd.

1 To make a small hat, CO 65 sts. To make a large hat, CO 75 sts.

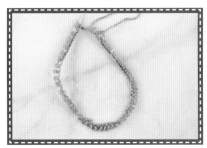

2 Place a st m on the right needle to mark the beginning of the rnd. Slip the m when you come to it. Join your CO row in the rnd, without turning work, making sure your sts aren't twisted.

3 Knit every st until your hat measures approximately 25.5 cm from the bottom. It will look like a tube. The bottom of your hat will curl up – make sure you measure it from the bottom of the roll (don't hold it down flat).

4 BO all sts. Cut yarn, leaving a 76-cm tail.

5 Sew the top together so that you have a rectangle shape that is open at the bottom.

To finish, pull the yarn through the corner. Turn the hat inside out. Pull the two corners together so they meet in the middle.

6 Sew the corners together. Weave in tails.

Knitting in the round vs. knitting flat

There are two kinds of knitting: knitting flat and knitting in the round. A scarf is knitted flat (back and forth, from needle to needle). A hat is usually knitted in the round (like a tube). The stitches are the same for flat and round knitting.

For flat knitting, you will turn your fabric at the end of the row and work back across to the other end. You can create flat fabric with any kind of needle (straight or circular and sometimes double pointed needles).

For knitting in the round, your fabric is made in one continuous row (like a spiral) without turning. For knitting in the round, you need circular needles or double pointed needles.

30

Stocking stitch

Reverse stocking stitch

In your knitting patterns, you will often see the terms "right side" and "wrong side". The right side of the fabric is the side that will be visible when you're wearing it. The wrong side is the part that is hidden (for example, the inside of a hat).

Often, the right side of a fabric is smooth and made up of knit stitches. This is called "stocking stitch" – St st. The wrong side of a fabric often looks like a bunch of little bumps (purls). This is called "reverse stocking stitch" - rev St st. When you are knitting stocking stitch in the round, you will knit all the stitches. When you are knitting stocking stitch flat, you will knit one row (right side – RS), turn, then purl one row (wrong side – WS).

Depending on the combination of knits and purls, your fabric might look a bit different. You will see that the Garter Stitch Cowl doesn't have a smooth side – both sides look the same and have ridges.

Bulky beanie

This hat knits up pretty quickly with a bulky yarn, so it makes a great gift. It is a good chance to practise your purl stitches and decreases. It uses a smaller needle size for the brim to make it snug so that the hat is more comfortable. You will change to dpns when closing up the top, so that your stitches don't stretch around your circular needle. This hat can be made in two sizes.

Materials

60 m / 100 g of a chunky weight yarn

6 mm 40-cm circular needles

6.5 mm 40-cm circular needles

stitch marker

large sewing needle

6 mm double-pointed needles

Skills

cast on, knit stitch, purl stitch, decreases

Work in the rnd.

1 For a small hat, CO 40 sts with the smaller needles. To make a large hat, CO 48 sts with the smaller needles.

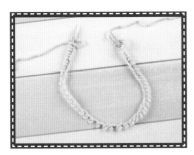

2 Pm for beg of rnd. Slip the m when you come to it. Join your CO row in the rnd, making sure your sts aren't twisted.

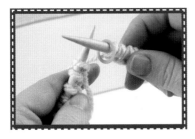

3 Knit 2 sts, purl 2 sts (K2, P2) to the end of the rnd. Rep this rnd until your hat measures approx 6.5 cm.

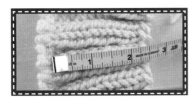

4 Small size only: Increase 1 st at the beg of the rnd, (K2, P2) across 20 sts, increase once more, (K2, P2) to the end of the rnd. 2 sts increased. 42 sts total.

5 Change to larger needles by knitting every stitch in the next rnd with the larger size and letting the smaller needles "dangle" to the back. At the end of the rnd, your smaller needles should be empty. Don't forget to replace the marker for the beginning of the rnd.

6 Continue knitting working in St st (knit every st) until your hat measures approximately 16.5 cm from the CO.

Tip:
Working purl sts on the brim prevents the fabric from curling up.

Decrease rnds:

Tip:
Two sets of remaining sts are given at the end of the rnds — one for the small size, one for the large size (in brackets).

Rnd 1: (K4, K2tog), rep to end of rnd. 35 (40) sts rem.

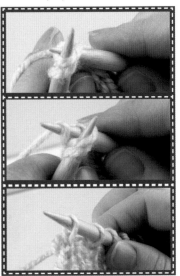

Rnd 2: Knit all sts.

Rnd 3: (K3, K2tog), rep to end of rnd. 28 (32) sts rem.

Rnd 4: Change to dpns and knit all sts.

Continued on the next page...

33

Rnd 5: (K2, K2tog), rep to end of rnd. 21 (24) sts remain.

Rnd 6: Knit all sts.

Rnd 7: (K1, K2tog), rep to end of rnd. 14 (16) sts remain.

Rnd 8: Knit all sts.

Rnd 9: (K2tog), rep to end of rnd. 7 (8) sts rem.

Cut yarn, leaving a 25.5-cm tail. Pull it through the remaining sts. Pull the tail through to the inside. Weave in all tails.

Tip:

When you see instructions in parentheses, you should repeat what is inside the parentheses according to the instructions that follow.

Frogging

Frogging got its name because you have to "rip it, rip it, rip it" (ribbit, ribbit, ribbit)! Frogging is also called "tinking". *Tink* is knit spelled backwards. As you might guess, this means that you take your fabric off the needles and pull the yarn out until you get back to where you need to be. If you want to put the fabric back on the needles, you can either try to place the loops back on the needles (but this can be tricky if the yarn is slippery and tends to unravel), or you can use the backwards knitting technique (see below) and unravel the row while at the same time, placing the loops onto the left needle.

Backwards knitting

If you have made a mistake recently in your knitting, you can just "back-up" a few stitches until the mistake is undone. This is accomplished by knitting in reverse. Insert your left needle into the next stitch just below your right needle from front to back, then let the "wrap" you just made fall away so that the stitch is now on the left needle.

Ribbed beanie

This hat is very stretchy and comfortable. You can knit a short version or a long version that folds up for an extra warm brim. This hat comes in two sizes.

Materials

200 m / 100 g of a worsted-weight yarn

4 mm 40-cm circular needles

4 mm double-pointed needles

stitch marker

large sewing needle

Skills

cast on, knit stitch, purl stitch, decreases

Work in the rnd

For the small hat, CO 88 sts.

For a large hat, CO 96 sts.

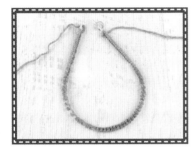

Pm for beg of rnd. Slip the m on the right needle to mark the beginning of the rnd. Slip the m when you come to it. Join your CO row in the rnd, making sure your sts aren't twisted.

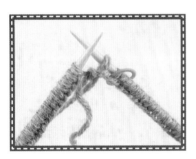

Knit 2 sts, purl 2 sts (K2, P2) to the end of the rnd. Rep this rnd until your hat measures approx. 15.25 cm from the CO for the short version or 25.5 cm from the CO for the long version.

Decrease rnds:

Note: Two sets of rem sts are given – one for the small size, one for the large size (in brackets).

Rnd 1: Knit all sts.

Rnd 2: (K6, K2tog), rep to end of rnd. 77 (84) sts rem.

Rnd 3: Knit all sts.

Tip:

Space stitches evenly on double pointed needles.

Rnd 4: (K5, K2tog), rep to end of rnd. 66 (72) sts rem.

Rnd 5: Knit all sts.

Rnd 6: (K4, K2tog), rep to end of rnd. 55 (60) sts rem.

Rnd 3: Change to dpns and knit all sts.

Rnd 4: (K3, K2tog), rep to end of rnd. 44 (48) sts rem.

Rnd 5: Knit all sts.

Rnd 6: (K2, K2tog), rep to end of rnd. 33 (36) sts rem.

Rnd 7: Knit all sts.

Rnd 8: (K1, K2tog), rep to end of rnd. 22 (24) sts rem.

Rnd 9: Knit all sts.

Rnd 10: (K2tog), rep to end of rnd. 11 (12) sts rem.

Cut yarn, leaving a 25.5-cm tail. Pull it through the rem sts. Pull the tail through to the inside. Weave in all tails.

Rainbow blanket

This blanket is made with garter stitch from corner to corner. It takes some perseverance, but when you are done you will be able to cuddle beneath a blanket you made yourself!

Materials

9 x 73 m / 50 g of a DK-weight yarn ("dishcloth" cotton) in 10 colours

OR

730 m / 510 g of any worsted-weight yarn

5.5 mm 81-cm circular needles

stitch marker

large sewing needle

Skills

cast on, knit stitch, yarn over, decreases

Special stitches:

YO (yarn over) - bring your live strand between the needles towards you, knit the next stitch as you normally would, making sure the strand wraps around the right needle to the back before you begin. This creates an extra stitch and a small (intentional) hole in your fabric.

38

Work back and forth (flat).

CO 2 sts.

Increases:

Row 1: K2.

Row 2: K1, CO 1 st, K1. 3 sts.

Row 3: Knit.

Row 4: K1, CO 1 st, K1, CO 1 st, K1. 5 sts.

Row 5: Knit.

Row 6: K1, CO 1 st, K3, CO 1 st, K1. 7 sts.

Row 7: Knit.

Row 8: K3, YO, K1, YO, K3. 9 sts.

Row 9: Knit.

Tip:

When you come to the YO, you will knit it just like it's a regular stitch.

Row 10: K3, YO, knit to the last 3 sts, YO, K3. 2 sts increased.

Place a safety pin on the side of the fabric where you are making the increases.

Rep Rows 9-10, changing colours if you want stripes until you have used half your yarn. You should have a large triangle.

Knit 1 row.

Decreases:

Row 1: K3, YO, K2tog twice, knit until you have 7 sts left, K2tog twice, YO, K3. 2 sts decreased.

Row 2: Knit.

Rep Rows 1 and 2 until you have 14 sts left.

Row 3: K3, YO, K2tog four times, YO, K3. 12 sts rem.

Rows 4, 6, 8, 10, 12: Knit.

Row 5: K3, K2tog, K2, K2tog, K3. 10 sts rem.

Row 7: K3, K2tog twice, K3. 8 sts rem.

Row 9: K2, K2tog twice, K2. 6 sts rem.

Row 11: K1, K2tog twice, K1. 4 sts rem.

Row 13: K2tog twice. 2 sts rem.

Cut yarn, leaving a 25.5-cm tail. Pull it through the rem 2 sts. Weave in all tails.

Tip:

Use a bulkier yarn for a larger blanket.

Striped wrist warmers

These wrist warmers are knitted flat and then sewn up the sides on two ends leaving a hole for your thumb. These come in two sizes, so there's something for everyone.

Materials

2 x 70 m / 50 g of a DK-weight yarn in two colours

3.5 mm straight needles

4 mm straight needles

large sewing needle

Skills

cast on, knit stitch, purl stitch, bind off, sewing ends together

Sometimes it's necessary to sew two pieces of knitted fabric together. There are many techniques for this, but here we will use the whip stitch.

1. Line up the fabric to where it should be sewn together. You might find it easier to pin it in place with safety pins. It is often easier to sew the seam with the "wrong side" of the fabric facing out. You can then turn it right side out when you are finished.

2. Thread your tail onto a large sewing needle.

3. Insert your needle into the first edge of the fabric from right to left and then through into the second edge. Pull the tail snug.

Repeat step 3 until you reach the end. You may choose to tie the tail off with a knot on the wrong side of the fabric, especially if it is a slippery yarn. Weave in the tail as you normally would.

Work back and forth (flat).
Make two.

With smaller needles, CO 30
(38) sts.

Cuff:

Set-up row: K3, *P2, K2*, rep
from * to * to last 3 sts, P2,
K1. Turn.

Rep this row until it measures
3.8 cm from cast on (bottom).

Hand:

Row 1 (RS): Change to larger
needles while knitting this
row. Turn.

Row 2 (WS): K1, purl to last
st, K1.

Attach colour B. Let colour A
hang to the side. Rep Rows 1
and 2 with colour B.

Rep the two rows alternating
between colour A and colour B
until you have 5 (6) stripes of
colour B. Cut colour B.

Rep Rows 1 and 2 once more
with colour A.

Change to smaller needles and
rep the Set-up row four times.

BO all sts. Cut yarn, leaving a
50-cm tail for sewing.

Tip:

When changing colours,
let the colour you just used
hang to the back; bring up
the new colour to the front
and begin knitting.

Finishing:

Turn the fabric so
the wrong side faces out
and pin together. Whip stitch
the edges together according
to the measurements on the
schematic, leaving a hole in
the middle for your thumb.
Weave in all tails.

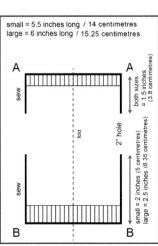

small = 5.5 inches long / 14 centimetres
large = 6 inches long / 15.25 centimetres

A   A
sew   both sizes = 1.5 inches (3.8 centimetres)
fold   2" hole
sew   small = 2 inches (5 centimetres) large = 2.5 inches (6.35 centimetres)
B   B

41

Kitty and bunny toys

These cute and cuddly toys are soft and friendly. They are knit in the round on double pointed needles, which may seem intimidating at first, but just remember that you only use two needles at a time, just like regular knitting.

Materials

2 x 75 m / 50 g of a worsted-weight yarn ("dishcloth" cotton) in two colours

Four sets of 4.5 mm double-pointed needles

stitch marker

large sewing needle

polyfill stuffing

black embroidery thread, and embroidery needle

Skills

cast on, knit stitch, increase, decrease, sewing ends together

M1 (make one) - increase. In this pattern, you can make your increase by casting on one stitch.

A note on knitting with double pointed needles: At first, it may look confusing with a bunch of needles in your hands, but you only use two needles at a time, letting the third and fourth needles hang to the back.

Start with stitches on three needles with the fourth "empty". Begin knitting the stitches on your first needle with the empty needle, just like you would if you were knitting flat. Eventually, your empty needle will be full of stitches and your first needle will now be empty. Continue like this, one needle at a time.

Work in the rnd.

Starting at the bottom, CO 30 sts. Leave a 38-cm tail for sewing up the bottom when you are done.

Divide your sts onto three dpns: 10-10-10.

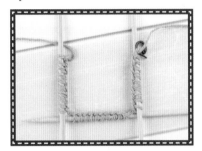

Join in the rnd. Make sure your sts aren't twisted. Pm for beg of rnd. Slip your m throughout.

Bottom:

Rnd 1: Knit.

Rnd 2: K2, M1, K13, M1, K2, M1, knit to end, M1. 4 sts increased. 34 sts.

Rnds 3-4: Knit.

Rnd 5: K2, M1, K15, M1, K2, M1, knit to end, M1. 4 sts increased. 38 sts.

Rnds 6-7: Knit.

Rnd 8: K2, M1, K17, M1, K2, M1, knit to end, M1. 4 sts increased. 42 sts.

Knit 12 rnds.

Top:

Rnd 1: K2, K2tog, K15, K2tog, K2, K2tog, knit to last 2 sts, K2tog. 4 sts decreased. 38 sts rem.

Rnd 2: Knit.

Rnd 3: K2, K2tog, K13, K2tog, K2, K2tog, knit to last 2 sts, K2tog. 4 sts decreased. 34 sts rem.

Rnd 4: Knit.

Rnd 5: K2, K2tog, K11, K2tog, K2, K2tog, knit to last 2 sts, K2tog. 4 sts decreased. 30 sts rem.

Rnd 6: Knit.

Rnd 7: K2, K2tog, K9, K2tog, K2, K2tog, knit to last 2 sts, K2tog. 4 sts decreased. 26 sts rem.

Rnd 8: Knit.

Rnd 9: K2, K2tog, K7, K2tog, K2, K2tog, knit to last 2 sts, K2tog. 4 sts decreased. 22 sts rem.

Rnd 10: Knit.

Rnd 11: K2, K2tog, K5, K2tog, K2, K2tog, knit to last 2 sts, K2tog. 4 sts decreased. 18 sts rem.

Knit 8 rnds.

Next Rnd: K2tog to the end. 9 sts rem.

Knit 1 rnd.

Continued on the next page...

Cut yarn, leaving a 25.5-cm tail. Pull it through the rem 9 sts. Pull the tail through to the inside.

Note: The ears are worked on 2 dpns, but you will work back and forth (flat).

Kitty ears (make two):

CO 4 sts.

Row 1: Purl.

Row 2: Knit.

Row 3: Purl.

Row 4: K2tog twice. 2 sts decreased. 2 sts rem.

Row 5: K2tog. 1 st decreased. 1 st rem.

Cut yarn and pull the tail through the rem st.

Bunny ears (make two):

CO 5 sts.

Knit 32 rows (16 "ridges").

Next: K2tog, K1, K2tog. 2 sts decreased. 3 sts rem.

Next: Knit.

Next: Slip the first st to your right needle without knitting it, K2tog, pass the slipped st over the st you just worked like you would to BO. 2 sts decreased. 1 st rem.

Cut yarn and pull the tail through the rem st.

Finishing:

Sew a simple face onto your toy with the embroidery needle and thread. Attach the ears to the top using a large sewing needle. Weave in all the tails. Stuff it with polyfill (but be careful not to over-stuff). Use a sewing needle to stitch up the bottom. Tie the tail off with a knot and pull it into the middle of the toy.

What to do when you make a mistake
Dropping a stitch

Dropping a stitch is probably one of the most common mistakes that a new knitter makes. This happens when a stitch falls off your needles without being knit. The stitch will unravel all the way to the bottom and your fabric will wind up with a big hole in it.

The easiest way to fix a dropped stitch is to use a crochet hook in a similar size to your needles. Find the spot where the stitch is still a loop. The strands above it will look like a ladder. Insert your crochet hook through the loop from front to back and grab it. Next, use the crochet hook to grab the "rung" above your loop. Pull this rung through the loop that is on your hook. Make sure your stitches aren't twisted. Continue climbing up your "ladder" until you get to the top. Place the stitch on the left needle, making sure it's facing the right way.

If you find a dropped stitch and it's too far down to pick up with a crochet hook, or you've already bound off your project, grab the stitch with a safety pin so it doesn't unravel further. Then, use an extra strand of yarn and a large sewing needle. Thread the strand through the loop and weave the ends of the strands into the back of your fabric – often you won't even notice!

45

Moss stitch bag

This bag makes a great gift or keep it for yourself to tote around your loot, books or a knitting project! It's knit in the round, which means some stitches are bound off and some are placed on a holder. The remaining stitches are knit flat (for the flap). A buttonhole is made and then the flap is bound off. The strap is then knit with the held stitches and sewn to the other side. Add a colourful button and enjoy!

Materials

2 x 202 m / 100 g of a worsted-weight yarn

4 mm 40-cm circular needles

small stitch holder, safety pin or scrap yarn

large button at least 4.5-cm wide

large sewing needle

Skills

cast on, knit stitch, purl stitch, bind off, sewing ends together

Work in the round.

Starting at the bottom, CO 100 sts. Leave a 38-cm tail for sewing up the bottom when you are finished.

Join in the rnd. Make sure your sts aren't twisted. Pm for beg of rnd. Slip your marker throughout.

Rnd 1: *K1, P1*, rep from * to * to end of rnd.

Rnd 2: *P1, K1*, rep from * to * to end of rnd.

Rep Rnd 1 and 2 until your bag measures 16.5 cm from the bottom.

Divide for Flap: K1, P1 across 8 sts, place these 8 sts on a stitch holder or safety pin, or mark with a scrap piece of fabric.

Remove m. Bind off next 50 sts. Continue in *P1, K1*, rep from * to * to last st, P1. Turn. These are the flap sts – you will now work back and forth.

Row 1 (WS): *P1, K1*, rep from * to * to end of row.

Row 2 (RS): *K1, P1*, rep from * to * to end of row.

Rep Rows 1 and 2 for 7.5 cm ending with a Row 1. RS should be facing for the next row.

Buttonhole:

Row 1 (RS): *K1, P1* across 18 sts, BO 6 sts, *P1, K1*, rep from * to * to end of row.

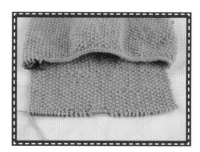

Row 2 (WS): *P1, K1*, rep from * to * to buttonhole gap, CO 6 sts, *P1, K1*, rep from * to * to end of row.

Row 3: *K1, P1*, rep from * to * to end of row.

Row 4: *P1, K1*, rep from * to * to end of row.

Rep Rows 3 and 4 three more times (8 rows total after buttonhole). BO all sts. Cut yarn, leaving a 25.5 cm tail.

Strap:

Move sts from holder to needles. Work back and forth. Attach yarn with RS facing.

Row 1 (RS): *P1, K1*, rep from * to * to end of row.

Row 2 (WS): *K1, P1*, rep from * to * to end of row.

Rep Rows 1 and 2 until strap measures 45 cm. BO sts and sew the strap to the other side of the flap (make sure it's not twisted!).

Finishing: Turn the bag inside out and sew up the bottom, making sure there are no holes and making sure the seam is in line with the flap. Sew the button in place. Weave in all tails.

Find out more

Knitting (I love Crafts), Rita Storey (Franklin Watts, 2017)

Knitting for Children, Claire Montgomerie (CICO Books, 2017)

Author bio

Kelly McClure has been knitting since the age of six and now designs knitting patterns and runs her own company, Bohoknits. Her designs have appeared in shops across North America and she has even taught knitting in Nepal. She usually knits all day long, but she also enjoys dyeing yarn and wandering around in the woods with her dog, Lois. She lives and works in Ontario, Canada.

Titles in this series

Crochet Projects That Will *Hook You*

Felting Projects You Won't Be Able to *Resist*

Knitting Projects You'll *Purl Over*

Seamless Sewing Projects